UNIVERSITY OF NORTH CAROLINA
STUDIES IN THE ROMANCE LANGUAGES AND LITERATURES
Number 65

LA CHANSON DE WILLAME
A CRITICAL STUDY

LA CHANSON DE WILLAME
A CRITICAL STUDY

BY

HOWARD S. ROBERTSON

CHAPEL HILL
THE UNIVERSITY OF NORTH CAROLINA PRESS

depósito legal: v. 3.146 - 1966

artes gráficas soler, s. a. — jávea, 30, — valencia (8)—1966

PREFACE

The impetus for this study came from my graduate seminar in mediaeval literature at the University of Alberta. I am grateful to the members of that seminar as well as to the following persons and institutions: Professors D. G. Mowatt of the University of Newcastle, Australia, and J. M. Ellis of the University of California who both kindly read my manuscript and offered many excellent suggestions, the University of Alberta which financed the research facilities and Mrs. June Panteluk who typed and corrected the various versions of the manuscript.

H. S. R.

This work has been published with the help of a grant from the Humanities Research Council of Canada using funds provided by the Canada Council.

Previous scholarship on the "Chanson de Willame"

The central questions in scholarship on the *Chanson de Willame* have been the date of authorship, the unity or composite nature of the poem, the geography and history of the work and finally, its literary value. While the dissertation of Mr. F. W. Nachtmann [1] provides us with a useful summary which perhaps excuses the present writer from the usual brief survey of scholarship, certain statements should be made. Critics have in the past largely approved the earlier dating of the *Chanson de Willame*; however, the date may now acceptably stand anywhere between 1140 and 1200 according to Jean Frappier and Mlle J. Wathelet-Willem on one hand and Duncan McMillan on the other. [2] This wide range has allowed considerable speculation on the position of the *Chanson* within the William Cycle and the search has continued apace for the "original" versions represented by the extant *Chanson de Willame*, *Chevalerie Vivien* and *Aliscans*. On the unity question, linguistic evidence, supposed differences of tone and stylistic evidence have all been adduced to prove the fundamental error involved in classing the two parts of the poem as one literary unity. Not all scholars have accepted this separation, although most have agreed to the proposition that the *Chanson de Willame* constitutes a rehandling of two separate themes (the Guillaume

---

[1] Francis W. Nachtmann, *A History of Studies of the Old French William Cycle*, dissertation, University of Illinois, 1958.

[2] Jean Frappier, *Les Chansons de Geste du Cycle de Guillaume d'Orange*, vol. I, Paris, 1955, pp. 150-56. Jean Wathelet-Willem. "Sur la date de la *Chançun de Willame*," *Les Lettres romanes*, VII (1953), 331-349. Duncan McMillan, *La Chanson de Guillaume*, S. A. T. F., Paris, 1950, II, 115 ff.

episodes and the Rainouart episodes) within a single redaction.³ The single most revealing study of the composition of the *Chanson de Willame* up to now has been the two-part article by Hugh A. Smith in 1913.⁴ No advance has been made on Mr. Smith's demonstration that the *lunsdi* portions of the text find parallels in the *Chevalerie Vivien* and the *Aliscans* while the *mercredi* and *joesdi* portions appear to be of the author's own invention and indeed owe much of their expression and language directly to the *lunsdi* portions or the sources thereof. To quote Mr. Smith's conclusion on the *Chanson*: "The purpose of the compilation called *La Chanson de Willame* is quite clear then. *It is an account of personal exploits or episodes of the heroes of the poem, with only enough of a general nature to give the proper setting or place of these exploits in the poem.*" ⁵ (Italics are Smith's.) One might conveniently add here the observation that Smith alone has made the slightest sense out of the refrains. Unfortunately, he ceases to examine the *Chanson de Willame* almost immediately as he continues in the next line following the above quotation: "This plan is certainly not the work of the original author," and plunges into a reconstruction of the text "common" to the *Chanson de Willame*, the *Chevalerie Vivien* and the *Aliscans* on pages 152-65. Mr. Smith's efforts greatly resemble later attempts to reconstruct the forebears of the *Chanson de Willame* instead of studying the poem in the form we have it. Typical of these studies is the recent effort of M. Jean Frappier, ⁶ who postulates a hypothetical *Chanson de Guillaume* variously described as "original," "primitive," and "authentic" and a similarly hypothetical *Chanson de Rainouart*. The *Chanson de Willame*, *Chevalerie Vivien* and *Aliscans* are then related on the basis of their possible connection with one or both of the two "originals." Anyone familiar with *Chanson de Willame* scholarship will recognize this fundamental pattern on which many changes have been rung since the dis-

---

³ We should add to the list given by Nachtmann the later article by Mlle Wathelet-Willem "Sur deux passages de la *Chanson de Guillaume*," *Moyen-Age*, LXV (1959), 27-40. See also note 13 below.

⁴ Hugh A. Smith, "The Composition of the *Chanson de Willame*," *Romanic Review*, IV (1913), 84-111, 149-165.

⁵ *Ibid.*, p. 98.

⁶ Frappier, *Les Chansons de Geste*, etc.

covery of the Edwardes manuscript in 1903. Specifically, M. Frappier states that the hypothetical *Chanson de Rainouart* is later than the *Couronnement Louis* because of the appeal to the king motif and also later than the *Charroi de Nimes* because of William's anger at Louis' ingratitude. *Aliscans* and the Rainouart episodes of the *Chanson de Willame* (henceforth called G^2, the first section being G^1) are different and independent versions of the "original" *Chanson de Rainouart*. M. Frappier then compares these two redactions in order to "préciser davantage l'esprit et le style de la *Chanson de Rainouart*, de discerner autant qu'il est possible le travail du remanieur..." [7] His conclusion is that *Aliscans* is a more intelligent, artistic and consistent, if less dramatic handling of the material than is G^2.

Now M. Frappier has succeeded in demonstrating that the *Aliscans* and G^2 are quite different, but he can hardly claim to have discovered anything about any hypothetical *Chanson de Rainouart*. He proposes his study in very modest terms: "...on ne peut se flatter de déterminer en toute certitude la besogne du remanieur, bien que divers indices permettent de le soupçonner, en plus d'un endroit, d'avoir abrégé son modèle, ou, inversement, d'avoir inséré des épisodes ou des scènes de son cru..." [8] and again, "Les bases de la comparaison se trouvent donc assez flottantes, mais ce n'est pas au point qu'elle soit vouée à un échec total et qu'elle ne guide pas vers la solution vraisemblable." [9] However, some thirty pages later, one finds this conclusion on the nature of the "authentic" *Chanson de Rainouart*: "On sait déjà qu'à nos yeux *Aliscans* est un renouvellement d'une *Chanson de Rainouart* conservée dans G^2 *avec plus ou moins de fidelité*." [10] (Italics mine.) Serious thought would indicate that in the absence of texts other than *Aliscans* and the *Chanson de Willame* and with the date of the latter possibly as late as 1200, it is difficult to see how any amount of comparison could result in the reconstruction of one specific "authentic" model or establish which reworking is more faithful to the hypothetical "original" with any

---

[7] *Ibid.*, p. 207.
[8] *Ibid.*, p. 205.
[9] *Ibid.*, p. 206.
[10] *Ibid.*, p. 237.

useful degree of accuracy. It is perhaps more important to say that M. Frappier's theorizing and reconstruction have absolutely nothing to do with the *Chanson de Willame* as a poem. Yet while speculation about an imaginary source leaves us none the wiser about the text at hand, M. Frappier persists in it. He explains away the comic scenes in G² by a reference to "l'esthétique médiévale qui ne répugnait pas au mélange des tons...", [11] after preparing us for this conclusion with the following assurance: "On sait qu'à notre avis la première épopée de Vivien et de Guillaume ignorait Rainouart et que l'énormité bouffonne de ses exploits est autre chose que le réalisme parfois plaisant ou caricatural de la *Chanson de Guillaume;* cela ne signifie point que certains traits dispersés dans G¹ n'ont pas servi à la composition du personnage; cela ne signifie pas non plus que l'emploi d'un comique trivial dans une chanson de geste ne se rattachait pas à une tradition littéraire et savante bien antérieure au XIIe siècle; on se tromperait aussi en expliquant Rainouart par une intention de parodie et de dénigrement: les trouvères de la *Chanson de Rainouart* et d'*Aliscans* ne songeaient pas le moins du monde à rabaisser l'idéal chevaleresque et chrétien." [12] The conclusions in this paragraph are based on M. Frappier's opinions about three hypothetical "originals" which may in fact not exist.

In explaining away the comedy of the *Chanson de Willame*, M. Frappier reveals that he shares the prevailing view of the *Chanson de Willame*: that it is a serious epic in the best mediaeval tradition. [13] William's role is that of the epic nobleman, the patriarch of chivalry, modeled on the Charlemagne of the *Chanson de Roland*. The suffering and dismay experienced by both men is typically explained by Mr. Frappier: "Ce pathétique, il faut l'avouer, est d'expression un peu larmoyante, conforme au ton très affectif de l'épopée médiévale; il provient en droite ligne

---

[11] *Ibid.*, p. 220.
[12] *Ibid.*, p. 219-20.
[13] One author not mentioned by Mr. Nachtmann is H. Dauer (*Der Kunstcharakter del Chancun de Willehelme*, dissertation, München, 1932), who sees a certain humour in the *Chanson de Willame* and regards William as a less-than-ideal leader, but makes no coherent statement on the comedy of the poem.

de la *Chanson de Roland,* car ici Guillaume est visiblement modelé d'après Charlemagne." [14] We are invited to view the exaggeration of both men's ages as "une manière naïve, qui a pu être efficace, de créer un surcroît d'émotion et d'attendrir l'auditoire sur le sort de ces héros chargés d'années et de deuils, témoins, acteurs et symboles d'une continuité historique faite d'un incessant combat; soudain, ces champions qui semblaient éternels, hors du temps, avouent leur lassitude, et l'accent humain de leur plainte touche nos cœurs." [15] Despite William's age and avowed weakness, he is still, in M. Frappier's view, "le bouclier et l'épée de la France entière... aucun autre personnage ne le relègue au second plan bien que le sacrifice de Vivien soit le moment le plus sublime du poème." [16] In his exposition of the *Chanson de Willame* (fuller than most and certainly typical in its orientation) M. Frappier goes on to point out Vivien as the essence of all the heroes who perished at Roncesvalles as well as the epic incarnation of the sacrificed Christ; he sees Tedbalt and Esturmi only as foils to the heroic Vivien and Girard, Gui as the expression of the *puer senex* topos, Guiburc as the model mediaeval chatelaine whose every action (even her deceit, presumably) is transposed "dans un registre épique, à la gloire de l'héroïne" [17] and Rainouart as an "outsider comique" who soon becomes "le héros favori." We might conveniently recall briefly M. Frappier's opinion on the comic elements in the *Chanson de Willame*: "Je ne découvre dans G^1 rien qui ressemble au burlesque de G^2 et aux exploits drolatiques de Rainouart." [18] Comparing the comic elements of our poem with those of the *Chanson de Roland,* he notes, "On voit... que le comique trivial n'est pas tout à fait absent de la *Chanson de Roland,* mais son accent de vengeance [19] est tel que nul ne voudra prétendre qu'il jure vraiment avec la tonalité

---

[14] Frappier, *Les Chanson de Geste,* etc., p. 181.
[15] *Ibid.,* p. 181.
[16] *Ibid.,* pp. 182-3. One must not overlook, however, the dominance of Rainouart in G^2.
[17] *Ibid.,* p. 178.
[18] *Ibid.,* p. 199.
[19] He speaks of the custody of Ganelon, vv. 1816-1829 in the Jenkins edition.

fondamentale, qui est celle d'un drame épique, il en va de même pour la *Chanson de Guillaume*." [20]

THE THEORETICAL BASIS OF THIS STUDY [21]

From the criticism made thus far of the prior scholarship on the *Chanson de Willame*, it emerges that there exists a need for a discussion of the difference in theoretical positions underlying this study and its predecessors. It seems clear that the traditional interpretation tends to regard the old French epic as something of an historical document which both comments on the nature of the society which created it and reflects the standards and beliefs of that society. The standard for this circular observation has been the first and possibly the greatest of these epics, the *Chanson de Roland*. The view that the *Roland* is a serious epic in the best sense of the term has been allowed to colour the vision of critics investigating later works and the conclusion has been drawn that mediaeval people were so imbued with epic standards (as inferred from the *Roland*) and so worshipped epic heroism (as embodied in the *Roland*) that none of them would have dreamed of being so disrespectful as to take a lighter view of chivalry.

Now the difficulty with the *Chanson de Willame* has always been its comic elements. While the obvious tack would have been to investigate the *Chanson de Willame* itself in order to determine exactly what it does say, the point of view outlined in the preceding paragraph has intervened to interpret this work as a serious traditional epic poem into which some comic elements crept because, as M. Frappier seems to imply, in the middle ages nobody minded. This point of view has discouraged any interpretation based on a reading of the text without reference to traditional "epic standards" or the "mediaeval mind" or the *Chanson de Roland*, despite the possible advantage accruing from a new interpretation which could enlarge the traditional concept "epic" and advance our appreciation of mediaeval literature as literature.

---

[20] Frappier, *Les Chansons de Geste*, etc., p. 200.
[21] We shall not review scholarship on the geographical and historical basis of the *Chanson de Willame*. The studies along this line have produced nothing of significance for the comprehension of the poem.

Since the prejudgment of the nature of the *Chanson de Willame* has precluded any unprejudiced reading of the text, critics have been forced to turn away from it and search out the "themes" and "meaning" of the text among external materials. The fact that the *Chanson de Willame* appears to have used two basic legends (William of Orange and Rainouart) has sent scholars off on the trail of the "original," "primitive," "authentic" sources (the genetic fallacy of the logicians) which have in some cases actually been reconstructed and then discussed. Parallel versions of the story have been investigated and compared with our text in order to interpret the various treatments of the material, and this activity has been preconditioned by the view that epic material was always taken seriously by mediaeval readers and audiences. This considerably reduced the value of any judgements reached by these methods. What actual reading of the text has occurred has been under the shadow of largely historical conclusions.

The sole manuscript which we possess of the *Chanson de Willame* is in a somewhat dilapidated state. The metrical structure of the poem has in the course of transmission been altered by unknown circumstances to the point where something over forty percent of the lines are hypermetric or incomplete. This unfortunate circumstance has been taken by most critics as a mandate to cast their eyes back to its imagined pristine state and to decide in advance that the text itself is unreliable wherever it presents difficulties to the interpreter. This sort of conclusion places the *Chanson de Willame* effectively outside the usual category of "literature" and authorizes the treatment of the poem from a non-literary standpoint which supplies from non-literary sources the remedy for any supposed deficiency. Now the present study is based on the totally different assumption that the text of the *Chanson de Willame* has a meaning. Doubtless the manuscript is in less than first-class shape, but the real point to be decided is: does the *Chanson de Willame* in the form in which we possess it reveal a total meaning worthy of consideration or does it not? Our answer to this question must be to assert the primacy of the text over external considerations such as history or the statements of other versions of the same legends, in short the primacy of what the text actually does say as opposed to a preconceived notion of what it should say. The way is then open to discover the themes of the *chanson* as products of the situations and characters, the whole being determined by the language of the text.[22]

Another problem peculiar to the *Chanson de Willame* (as indeed to many other texts) is the question of what has been called "unity." Hitherto, the unity of the text has been equated, or rather confused, with the unity or disparity of the possible sources much along the lines of "did the poet of the *Chanson de Willame* actually join two poems together or did he write the whole *chanson* as a piece?" The obvious answer would be that the *Chanson de Willame* looks like the union of two separate legends, but the real point is that it does not matter. What matters is whether or not the poem is a thematic whole; if the poet did join two legends, is the result cohesive? Are the themes sustained? Does the poem, in short, form an "artistic unity?" The difference between the two points of view revolves around the approach to literature involved and indeed the definition (however vaguely expressed) of literature. Does the investigation of the source(s) of a text reveal anything central to the text? Or must the text itself be the focal point of first consideration from which all other matters may arise? The present study operates on the basis of the latter theoretical position, since it alone provides an opportunity of discovering the meaning of the *Chanson de Willame* as it stands in the Edwardes manuscript.

One final problem central to the *Chanson de Willame* is the question of chivalry, its hierarchy, traditions and qualities. This study will advance the theory that the view of chivalry revealed in the *Chanson de Willame* is irreverent and atypical, involving as it does both satire and parody. The satire and parody are not, however, directed so much against one particular epic as against

---

[22] The search for respectable antecedents is endless. This modest study finds itself sharing the point of view of Robert Graves on the *Iliad* (*The Anger of Achilles,* Cassell, 1959) and D. G. Mowatt on the *Nibelungenlied* (*The Nibelungenlied,* Everyman's Library, 1962, and "Studies towards an interpretation of the Nibelungenlied," *German Life and Letters,* XIV (1961), no. 4, pp. 257-70). Like the latter, it questions the contribution of the historical approach with its worship of the "serious" past and the search for sources with its unproductive circle of hypotheses.

the whole idea of epic chivalry. Statements will frequently be made to the effect that the poem tends to explode the myth of a chivalry which no longer possessed the semblance of being a fact of history. It would not do to have the issue clouded by the argument that the clear distinction must at all times be drawn between the "chivalry" of the epic and that of the courtly romance. It is precisely the validity of this distinction that is under question and it may well have to be rejected or modified on the grounds that features common to the knight in both genres cannot be ignored because of the undoubted differences in subject matter, character, situation and language which exist between the two. Occasional references to courtly romances in this study are intended to be viewed from this standpoint and the major point still stands that the *Chanson de Willame* directs its satire in the main against the chivalry of the Old French epic.

Let us mention our conclusions which we must then substantiate. Far from being the "tragédie épique en deux actes"[23] of Ferdinand Lot or the "œuvre originale à un niveau épique très comparable à celui de la *Chanson de Roland*"[24] of M. Frappier, the *Chanson de Willame* has all the appearance of a late composite version of many elements of the William of Orange legend arranged to explode the myth of the superhuman heroes of chivalry by showing the fundamental contradiction of the theory of epic warfare and its practice. The elements of this theme, found throughout the poem, reveal a pattern which argues strongly for the artistic unity of the *Chanson de Willame*, whatever its sources may well have been. Vivien, the epic hero in the style of Roland, pursues an impossible ideal through to his own destruction; Tedbalt and Esturmi are the realities of the battlefield in epic trappings; William, the mighty conqueror famed in song and story, turns out to be a tired old man living on his laurels who is successively rescued from disaster by his wife, a fifteen-year-old nephew and a giant kitchen boy who just happens to be Guiburc's

---

[23] Ferdinand Lot, *Etudes sur les légendes épiques françaises*, Paris, 1958, p. 251. In fairness, it should be said that Lot is speaking only of vv. 1-1980; he rejects the second part of the poem as a "appendice malencontreux."
[24] Frappier, *Les Chansons de Geste*, etc., p. 201.

long lost brother and therefore noble after all. The *Chanson de Willame* contains in greater or lesser proportion most of the clichés of the epic; the great exception is the lack of *merveilleux chrétien,* unless you interpret v. 1858 ("Ço fu grant miracle que nostre sire fist") [25] with some capital letters. The study maintains that we owe to some unknown author of the period 1140-1200 a mosaic composition which, albeit often roughly and unevenly, presents an untraditional and often comic view of the legend of William of Orange and the myth of chivalry. Through whatever inconsistencies the Edwardes manuscript may possess, there emerges clearly the idea that a later twelfth-century Frenchman could understand that the flowering of chivalry was not all it seemed. Let us examine the significant episodes.

The Tedbalt-Esturmi Episodes

After the introduction of eleven lines, we move directly into the narrative as the author introduces his first two specimens of knighthood: Tedbalt and Esturmi. They are returning from vespers so drunk "que plus n'i poet estre" (v. 32) when the dreadful news of Deramed's invasion is frankly and briefly told by a messenger. Tedbalt immediately seeks advice. The messenger advises combat; Vivien advises sending for William's help which Tedbalt, as an honoured count, can do without shame. However, Esturmi, rather a more belligerent sort of drunkard, reminds his friend that William is a glory hunter who can show up with five, four or even three men at a battle and posterity will award him the victory. (vv. 59-67) He counsels immediate combat on their own. Hearing the traditional hero slandered, Vivien, shortly to be revealed as the "perfect knight," defends this symbol of his value system. (vv. 70-74) Esturmi replies that he is tired of hearing William praised and his own men disparaged. (vv. 75-77) Tedbalt is deaf to the sincere plea advanced by Vivien and, his courage fortified by wine, remarks that Vivien is only calling for help

---

[25] All references to lines of the poem will be taken from the McMillan edition.

because he fears battle. (vv. 78-79) Vivien's heated reply is lost on the drunken Tedbalt who calls for more wine to toast his best counsellor, Esturmi. Boasting like the typical drunkard, Tedbalt sets *primes* for the hour of departure and adds

> De set liwes en orrat l'em les criz,
> Hanstes freindre e forz escuz croissir. (vv. 92-93)

While Vivien goes to rest, the two boon companions settle down to drink.

Of the first ninety-six lines, over two-thirds are devoted to this inauspicious beginning to the campaign. Tedbalt and Esturmi, the Falstaff and Bardolph of an earlier age, go through the motions of Christian gentility at vespers, emerge to meet the news of war through a drunken haze, picture themselves undertaking a battle on their own, proffer insults right and left, toast each other as the best of companions and finally set about drinking themselves into a stupor in preparation for the morrow.

And the morrow comes. At dawn, Tedbalt is sobered considerably by the sight of Saracens so numerous that they cover the ground. "Deus!" says he looking out the window, "iço que pot estre?" (v. 104) Vivien, not too dissatisfied with Tedbalt's reaction, comments that now Tedbalt is sober and concludes "Ore atendrun nus Willame al curb niés." (v. 116) The comedy of confusion is continued, however, by Esturmi who comes riding up to compare notes with Tedbalt. Esturmi inquires,

> Ber, ne te menbre del repeirer de vespres,
> De Deramed e de la dure novele?
> Respunt Tedbald: 'Ai jo mandé Willame?
> —Nenil, bels sire, car il ne puet a tens estre.
> Par mi le col t'en oras herseir dehé,
> Si tu mandoues Willame al curb niés. (vv. 125-30)

Once having gotten the situation straight, Tedbalt decides that his sole course is to try to see matters through. He arms and rides out to fight.

Not content with having presented Tedbalt and Esturmi as typical drunkards, the poet follows them out to the field where it quickly becomes apparent that Tedbalt has never seen a

battlefield before. He mistakes the fleet for the encampment
(v. 152) and, when corrected, asks Vivien to reconnoitre the camp
for him. (vv. 160-62) Vivien refuses to degrade himself by count-
ing the enemy; William taught him to keep his helmet down right
to the field of combat. (vv. 163-67) The helmet, restricting the
knight's vision is an appropriate symbol here for the restricted
view taken by Vivien as he hews to the letter of knightly conduct
and never deviates from the stubborn premises which Roland and
the peers exemplified.[26] We shall see later where this attitude leads. Vivien suggests that Tedbalt is free, however, to decide
whether to fight or wait and send for help, since he is the leader
and can claim the responsibility of his men as an excuse. (vv.
168-78) Taking better counsel now, Tedbalt goes to survey the
situation for himself. His reaction to the overwhelming odds
usually encountered in an epic situation is immediate and atypical:

> Ki ore ne s'en fuit, tost i purrad mort gisir;
> Alum nus ent tost pur noz vies garir. (vv. 194-95)

In vv. 196-201, Tedbalt orders Vivien to lead the army back
down the valley, keeping out of sight of the enemy, while he
goes for William. One has the distinct impression that Tedbalt
wants to get out of danger as quickly as possible, leaving Vivien
to look after the army. Vivien's only reply is singularly inappro-
priate to the circumstances but very much in character: "Conbat

---

[26] Compare the following from Hartmann von Aue, *Erec* (Hans Naumann
& Hans Steinger, eds., *Hartmann von Aue: Erec/Iwein*, Leipzig, 1933):

> "von wiu kam daz diu frouwe baz
> beide gehôrte unde sach?"
> ich sage iu von wiu daz geschach.
> diu frouwe reit gewaefens bar:
> dâ was er gewâfent gar,
> als ein guot ritter sol.
> des gehôrter noch gesach sô wol
> ûz der îsenwaete
> als er blôzer taete.
>
> (vv. 4151-59)

Vv. 4157-59 especially illustrate the restrictive nature of knightly armour
(the helmet) and serve to point up the appropriateness of this particular
symbolism.

t'en ber, sis veinteruns, jol te plevis." (v. 207) The standard epic encouragement is scarcely what Tedbalt's terror requires. "Tedbalt," says Vivien, "you should measure up to William;" (vv. 208-11) but Tedbalt has a much more realistic appreciation of his own capabilities. The Saracens, having seen Tedbalt on the hill, realize that the French are nearby and move up onto terra firma to mount a charge 100,000 strong. The poet takes thirty lines to describe the magnificence of the charging Saracens in terms calculated to strike terror into the cowardly and stir the blood of the brave. (vv. 212-39) Vivien, predictably, praises the Saracen horses, foretells the death of cowards at Archamp, recommends faith in God and reassures his hearers with promises of victory. (vv. 241-51) Tedbalt has evidently not been listening to this epic encouragement, for he asks both Vivien and Esturmi what they think should be done. (vv. 252-55) Esturmi replies quite succinctly that whoever does not flee will die. (v. 256) Vivien's insulting "Now I hear a dog speaking" (v. 258) is lost on Tedbalt who reverses his lance, tears off the ensign and tramples it into the mud saying,

> Mielz voil, enseigne, que flanbe te arde del ciel
> Qu'en bataille me reconuissent paen. (vv. 275-76)

With the other cowards, he flees at the first blows.

The next 49 lines (vv. 279-327) are devoted to Vivien's rallying around himself the brave who have remained on the field with him even though they owe him no feudal loyalty. The sight of the chevalier nailing a makeshift ensign to his lance (even with three gold nails which are somehow readily available) and taking command of the valorous while the cowards flee is a stirring picture indeed, but with their cry of "Munjoie!" echoing in our ears we turn back immediately to watch the flight of the badly frightened Tedbalt. (vv. 328-404) The contrast inherent between the description of the brave and loyal knights and the flight of Tedbalt is heightened by the figurative and symbolic language employed in each situation by the poet. Beginning with the description of Vivien and his knights, the poet chooses an exceptionally noble figure:

> Si cum li ors s'esmere fors de l'argent,
> Si s'en eslistrent tote la bone gent;

> Li couart s'en vont od Tedbald fuiant,
> Od Vivien remistrent tuit li chevaler vaillant,
> (vv. 328-31)
> ... ...
> Si cun li ors fors de l'argent s'en turne,
> Si s'en eslistrent tut li gentil home.
> (vv. 333-34)

Gold as the symbol of the loyal knights is distinguished from silver as the bravest are distinguished from the brave. The human alchemy of vv. 330-31 reflects the chemical operation of v. 328. And the operation is repeated in vv. 333-34. The description of the knights fighting "en la pointe" follows. But as the attention is turned from the glory of battle to the shame of Tedbalt's flight, the language descends several levels to record the most shameful of possibilities as Tedbalt, running into a corpse dangling from a gibbet, soils his saddle blanket. Raising up, he kicks the offensive object away and tries to persuade Girard, his squire, to recover it. Girard's answer, "E jo que fereie quant cunchie est tote?" (v. 354) strikes the lower note which makes the contrast complete.

Tedbalt is tricked by Girard into coming within arm's length; promptly the latter unhorses him, strips off his armour and sends the stupified knight galloping off on his own palfrey. Tedbalt's flight is blocked by a palisade which is too high to leap; unable to tear out a couple of the posts, Tedbalt has the choice of following the palisade back in the direction of the battle or over a hill through a flock of sheep. He chooses the latter course, catches a sheep in his stirrup and so heedless is his flight that he arrives at Bourges with the sheep's head still stuck in the stirrup. The poet cannot resist the comment "Une tel preie ne portad mes gentilz hom." (v. 402) To complete the portrayal of the disgraced knights, Girard meets Esturmi fleeing in his turn. The erstwhile squire remonstrates with him and finally unhorses him with "un curteis mot." (v. 422).

Clearly, this entire episode of 429 lines deals with an account of the deeds of the anti-knight — the anti-hero whose drunkeness, boasting, jealousy, fear, avarice, disregard of his fellows and panic-stricken flight are the antithesis of the tradition of Roland and the twelve peers. Unknown these characteristics may be to the literary myth of the ideal hero, the myth of a Charlemagne or a William of Orange, but the common sense and even the living memory of a twelfth-century audience drawn from all classes are quite another matter. Tedbalt is the combination of debauchery, boastfulness, inexperience and cowardice known to every period of history. The sheer pathetic comedy of his headlong flight can be appreciated by any audience which recognizes the limits of individual capacity and has tired of the sterility of tales of superhuman courage and endurance repeated over and over again. When the trumpet sounds for battle, there are many Tedbalts in the ranks. Their conduct is despicable (though perhaps sensible), pathetic and humorous in a macabre way. These are very human reactions, as real to a mediaeval audience as to us, just as the prowess of a Roland, a Charlemagne or a William could appear unreal to twelfth and twentieth-century audiences alike.

Vivien, Girard and the Theory of Knighthood

The cowards having fled, the field is left to Vivien in whom we have already noted the attributes of the ideal epic knight. It remains for us to observe the characteristics of his leadership since it is primarily as leader that he now appears. He shouts epic encouragement to his men:

> Ferez, seignurs, od voz espees beles!
> Ferez, Franceis, desrumpez ceste presse!
> (vv. 451-52)

In verse 453-54 he says he has heard William or Louis coming:

> Jo ai oi Liwés u Willames,
> S'il sunt venuz, l'estur ne durra gueres.

One is almost surprised that the editors have not suspected a lacuna here so ready are they to find them on slimmer evidence. Possibly the more reasonable interpretation is that Vivien is indulging in a little "kidding of the troops," not an unusual practice, as we shall note again. In vv. 463-64, Vivien rebukes Girard for speaking ill of Tedbalt: "Par vostre lange ne seit prodome honiz." The parallel of Roland's rebuke to Olivier (vv. 1024-27, Jenkins edition) for speaking ill of Ganelon, implying as it does a comparison of the latter with Tedbalt, only serves to place Vivien in a ridiculous light. Besides shouting encouragement to his men, Vivien wrings his hands and "regrets" William (v. 479), regroups his men shouting that they will await William there (vv. 483-86), comforts the wounded by telling them that they will have no medical aid (vv. 501-02, a message taken up by the others in vv. 537-38), and in the style of archbishop Turpin, promises salvation to all those who die in combat. (vv. 545-47) It is at this point that the common sense of the remaining knights begins to assert itself. Offers of vengeance, death, salvation and vain pledges of victory coupled with a vague hope that God may send them William or Louis (neither of whom has been sent for) somehow fail to inspire the twenty remaining men. Vivien's assurance that "...ben les veintruns solunc la merci Deu" (v. 573) elicits the reply that God has forgotten them. (v. 574) Many of them add that Vivien is a madman if he thinks to lead twenty men into battle against 500,000; if the Saracens were only pigs it would still be impossible to slaughter 500,000 of them in a whole month! (vv. 575-79) Despite Vivien's remonstrances recalling their oath to their fallen comrades and his own oath never to retreat, they leave him, returning only when they see that all escape is cut off. (vv. 611-19).

Manifestly, the path of knightly conduct leads but to slaughter. The sum of Vivien's leadership is vain hopes and assurances of victory, blind faith in raw courage and a certain confusion in the reports given out as to whether William is coming in reinforcement. The strategy seems to be to hold on to an ideal even though it means to lose the battle and to be content to lose both battle and war provided that the myth of chivalry is maintained intact. Even the knightly have a certain proportion of brains, however, and Vivien's empty leadership only wins the knights' loyalty when despair leaves them no other choice. The decision to send for William comes, of course, too late. And the decision is approached in a most indecisive fashion as Vivien couches his proposition to Girard in imperfect subjunctives ("Amis Girard, si jo te ossasse quere / Que par la lune me alasses a Willame?" vv. 633-634) after inquiring rather obtusely about Girard's health and the state of his arms and horse. (vv. 623-32) The long passage (vv. 635-678) setting forth the reasons why William should come is largely a rehearsal of Vivien's past achievements on Williams's behalf along with reminders of how much William owes his vassal. The full epic treatment flies in the face of the situation but fits admirably the character of Vivien, who follows knightly precedent to the very end.

Comparisons between Vivien and Roland have not been lacking. Again, M. Frappier supplies us with one which is typical in taking as its theme the glorification of the chivalric hero. [27] Now the only qualities common to both heroes (and admirable to a point in them) are personal courage and prowess on the battlefield. While Roland is indeed faced with an unavoidable rearguard action and must engage a foe who has already seen him and is preparing to attack, he nevertheless does stubbornly refuse reasonable aid out of an ill-conceived pride and only gives in under the pressure of a desperate, not to say hopeless, situation. This unfounded and really senseless pride has been glorified by the name of "prouesse" *(fortitudo)* while the countering common sense attitude has been called "prudence" *(sapientia)*. M. Frappier conveniently finds both these qualities in Vivien [28] and he is absolutely correct. However, M. Frappier admits that "quelque flottement subsiste sans doute dans le personnage de Vivien." [29] Perhaps this is due to the fact that the comparison was not carried far enough. Vivien, faced at first with a situation where choices are possible and strategy is appropriate, advises the strategy of reinforcement. This is *sapientia*. However, insulted by the slanderous remarks of the drunken Tedbalt (whom he ought to have ignored), Vivien withdraws (inside his helmet as it were) and stubbornly refuses to take the responsibility for decisions even when he knows that Tedbalt is wrong. After Tedbalt's flight, instead of instituting the strategy he had at first advised, he holds to the model education he has received and leads all who will follow into a hopeless battle with never a thought of reinforcement. This is *fortitudo*. Once in the battle, Vivien exhibits the prowess and courage of

---

[27] Frappier, *Les Chansons de Geste*, etc., pp. 183 ff.
[28] *Ibid.*, p. 185.
[29] *Ibid.*

the twelve peers. Also, he displays the faith of Archibishop Turpin and makes to his men the promise which the famous cleric made at Roncesvalles: that all who fight for the right cause and die in the strife will reap eternal salvation. (vv. 545-47) One knight figure thus bears the burden of sustaining the epic tradition against the realities of Tedbalt and Esturmi, of William and Girard and the caricature of prowess displayed by Gui and Rainouart. Laden with every cliché in the book, Vivien goes down to a glorious, but needless, defeat. The myth of the leader whose strength and courage will overcome hopeless odds and whose example will inspire men to submit to useless slaughter is nothing less than the myth of the superman. Even Vivien's knights see this truth and revolt. He does not succeed as did Roland in controlling and inspiring his knights. It remains only to realize that the man of the twelfth century could regard the superman much as we might regard d'Artagnan — a colourful but improbable figure with more courage than good sense and more regard for a dying or dead code of ethics than for the well-being of those dependent upon him. We admire d'Artagnan's swordsmanship and are breathless at his daring. But we know he does not exist.

As if to reinforce the contrast between reality and poetry, the poet leaves Vivien before his death to follow Girard to Orange. Once away from the battle and the influence of the ideal knight, Girard, who only that morning was a squire, succumbs to the forces of nature. Thirst, hunger and heat all take their toll and, piece by piece, Girard throws away the cumbersome armour, retaining only his sword, which he uses as a pilgrim would his staff. (vv. 703-41) The exhausted warrior, his horse dead, walking home from a lost battle, is a sympathetic figure and was likely not an unfamiliar one. While it might be interesting to note in this juxtaposition a contrast between the supposed glory of the battlefield and the sad reality of the results, we may press on to consider the death of Girard in the second battle of Archamp — a death curiously paralleled by that of Guischard, Guiburc's converted pagan nephew recently dubbed a knight by William. Since this passage has no parallel in either the *Aliscans* or the *Chevalerie Vivien*, we are faced with a direct interpretation of the text if we wish to understand it at all.

The Christian-born Girard, mortally wounded, tells William that he does not wish to be borne away from the field or have his wounds tended; rather he asks only to be given a drink of clear wine (or, failing that, of water from the nearby polluted brook), to be set on his horse sword in hand and he will fight on. (vv. 1150-61) Guischard, the converted pagan, also mortally wounded, replies to William's sympathetic inquiry in language very similar to Girard's that he does not wish to be carried away or have his wounds attended. If he were set on his horse and given a drink of clear wine (or water from the same brook), says he, he would never bear arms for William again. Ceasing to believe in the Christian God, he would go to Cordres, his native city:

> Car si jo eusse Mahomet merciez,
> Ja ne veisse les plaies de mes costez.
> (vv. 1198-99)

The ironical implication of his words is clear: had he never become involved in Christian knightly society, he would not now be on the losing side of the desperate French chivalry. While the Christian Girard dies as a knight should, eager and fighting to the end, the convert returns to his old religion when he realizes the foolishness that Christian knighthood has led him into. True to his training through *chanson de geste* and example, Girard remains enthusiastic and blind to the end; Guischard faces the plain facts as his life ebbs away and shrugs off the foolish heroics of chivalric propaganda along with the God of the Christian paladin. William reviles the relapsed knight, but, fearing Guiburc's reaction if he breaks his promise of vv. 1033-37, he is forced into the ignominious position of having to carry him back to Orange while he presumably leaves behind the noble Girard of whom we hear no more. There is yet another implication in the death of Guischard. It bears directly on the oft-made comparison between William and his "epic model" Charlemagne whose mass conversions (one hundred thousand pagans after the capture of Saragosse) are the traditional mark of the epic conqueror. William seems far from the model Christian conqueror as his adopted and recently dubbed nephew rejects the faith of the French chivalry.[30]

Guiburc — the source of strength

A close examination of the *Chanson de Willame* reveals the rather surprising fact that the principal figure, William of Orange, though ostensibly in the foreground throughout most of the poem, never initiates any action, performs in the main badly when called upon to exercise his prerogatives of leadership and is only credited with a few stock epic achievements during his three battles. The actions of "Willame Ferebrace" (v. 479) are mainly dictated and his reputation and life are saved by his wife Guiburc, his nephew Gui and his giant aide Rainouart. M. Frappier's description of Guiburc as a dutiful wife and a model chatelaine of epic nobility [31] hardly squares with a detailed examination of Guiburc's actions.

From the first, Guiburc takes the very initiative one would expect of her husband. Her immediate response to Girard's plea for aid is decisive and unequivocal:

> Respunt Guiburc: "Pur nient en parlez.
> Secor le, sire, ne te chalt a demander.
> Se tu l'i perz, n'avras ami fors Deu."
> (vv. 1004-06)

Baldly, she lectures William on his knightly duty, "Secor le, sire, ne te chaut a demurer." (v. 1030) Probably in an effort to build up William's ego, likely in order to shame him into proper action, she offers him her own newly dubbed nephew, charging William with the responsibility of taking Guischard to battle and bringing him back alive or dead. She adds a small threat, "Si nel me renz, ne girras mes entre mes braz" (v. 1036) and William agrees immediately.

Even before William's return from his first defeat, Guiburc has apparently foreseen the possibility of a second expedition

---

[30] See pp. 40-41 below for fuller discussion of the Willame-Charlemagne comparison.
[31] Frappier, *Les Chansons de Geste*, etc., p. 178.

and has therefore gathered some 30,000 men together and is keeping them occupied with food, drink and entertainment when, as expected, William returns alone and defeated. On this occasion, however, Guiburc provides more than advice and troops. Evidently, she has thought the situation out and reached the conclusion that the unadorned facts of the recent disaster will not generate much enthusiasm for battle among her 30,000 guests. Asking William's permission to lie about the situation seems largely a formality as Guiburc goes up the stairs to the great hall with William's shouts of encouragement following after, "Ore va, Guiburc, mentez asez par mun gré." (v. 1360) One must wonder at the unashamed propaganda she employs to rally a following for William. Preparing the way with an obvious truth ("Ja est venue Willame.../ Tut sains e salfs..." vv. 1366-67), she proceeds in the best propaganda style with two enormous lies ("Si ad vencu la bataille champel / E ocis le paien Deramé." vv. 1368-69). While admitting one small complication ("Mais d'une chose ad malement erré; / Il ad perdu sun noble barné." vv. 1370-71), she hurries over the annihilation of William's army to emphasize the booty left in the disabled ships and guarded by only 10,000 Saracens. (vv. 1379-87) As added inducement, Guiburc indicates William's willingness to be generous with his own lands and possessions and offers the knights their choice from among 160 maidens presently in her household. Scholars have wondered that the lie is never mentioned again, that Guiburc and William never suffer as the result of so prodigious a falsehood. Seen in the context of a pattern of standard, traditional (dare one say "historical"?) propaganda, the answer would seem to be that the lie was never intended to be caught up. The audience expected the lie as they expected the other lies which led men to battle in those days as we in our turn have lies to lead them to battle now. Patriotism, honour, allegiance to lords, ideals, codes, all take their place alongside the more telling enticements of booty, wealth, land, wives. The whole scheme is carefully contrived with the audience sitting in the middle of the spectacle. The poet concludes the scene with the fatalistic observation not untinged with sarcasm:

> Tel s'aati de choisir la plus bele
> Qui en l'Archamp perdi puis la teste.
>
> (vv. 1398-99)

With each defeat, Guiburc is obliged to take a more decisive role and assume wider responsibility in her husband's affairs. After his second defeat, William is ready to retire from the world ("La devendrai hermites ordené, / E tu devien noneine, si faz tun chef veler." vv. 2418-19) Guiburc's refusal is firm and unhesitating;

> Sire, dist ele, ço ferum nus assez
> Quant nus avrom nostre siecle mené!
>
> (vv. 2420-21)

Carrying her positive attitude further, she advises a mission to Louis to secure aid, even mapping out the strategy which William is to follow.

> Sire Willame, al Dampnedeu congié!
> Par main a l'albe munte sur tun destrer,
> Dreit a Loun pense de chevalcher
> A l'emperere qui nus solt aver chiers,
> Qui del socurs nus vienge ça aider.
> E s'il nel fait, si li rendez sun fee;
> Mar en tendré un jur un demi pee.
> Met en provende et tei et ta moiller,
> U a sa table nus laist, pur Deu, manger
> A chascun jur de sun pain dous quarters.
>
> (vv. 2422-31)

The instruction is typical of Guiburc. Not only does she outline the main strategy and its terms, but she spells out in telling detail the alternatives. If no aid is forthcoming, Louis can either put them, man and wife, on the dole or allow them daily at his table to eat their allotted "dous quarters" of his bread. The message contains a striking contrast of terms whose significance should reach the king. Typically, William only delivers the obvious part of the message. (vv. 2535-37) He readily agrees to this desperate measure, however, adding that Guiburc's advice has always been good.

E dit Willame: "Jol ferai mult iree,
Mais tun conseil en dei jo creire ben;
En plusurs lius m'ad eu mult grant mester."
(vv. 2432-34)

Guiburc's last real contribution as the power behind William is to reconcile him and Rainouart when the latter has already rebelled and is on the point of desertion. The role is natural for her, since she has already established good relations with this likely-looking warrior prior to the battle, girding him with a sword although he refused knighthood and preparing him a bed. (vv. 2822-63) Indeed, it is for Guiburc's sake that Rainouart refrains from slaughtering more of the French. (vv. 3463-65) Once again, Guiburc makes the overture to Rainouart and asks for reconciliation; there is manifestly no time to consider William's feelings in the matter. It seems plain that Guiburc is the mainspring of William's action. No campaign is undertaken, no army led out, no policy or strategy decided except by her. She provides William with the necessities for a successful campaign; if defeat ensues, the fault lies not with her.

The defeat brings out Guiburc's second function — as the model of common sense and practical attitudes, the voice of criticism and even sarcasm. While her readiness to offer unsolicited advice, lecture William on his duty, and supply troops constitutes an implied criticism, after a defeat the implicit becomes explicit. William's return to Orange after each of his first two battles involves a porter scene. The first such scene, occurring in the *jeudi* portion (vv. 1282-87), where William asks Guiburc how long she has been his gatekeeper, is obviously based on the second in the last *lunsdi* portion (vv. 2214 ff.) which finds a counterpart in *Aliscans*. (vv. 1571 ff.) Hugh A. Smith noticed this and observed that while the whole episode seems pointless on the surface, it does serve to enlarge the role of Guiburc.[32] Examining this further, we note that Guiburc takes the opportunity to comment during the first scene on the few knights William has left (i.e., none) ("Sire Willame, poi en remeines chevalers!" v. 1287) and relate her duties as gatekeeper directly to the shortage of

---

[32] Smith, "The Composition of the *Chanson de Willame*," p. 90.

manpower. While Guiburc laments with William and comforts him over the loss of his knights, she shortly assumes the critical stance and once again lectures him on his knightly duty. (vv. 1319-27) The second porter scene provides more scope for Guiburc as critic as she rejects the notion that William has botched his second expedition and is once again returning in defeat despite her best efforts. Her patience exhausted by a second inglorious return, she lectures this apparent stranger on what she expects from the mighty William of Orange.

> Si vus fuissez Willame al curb niés,
> Od vus venissent set mile homes armez,
> Des Frans de France, des baruns naturels;
> Tut entur vus chantassent ces juglers,
> Rotes e harpes i oist hom soner.
> (vv. 2244-48)

In the midst of his explanation, Guiburc notices the Saracens in the distance and sends this improbable stranger off to prove himself by chasing them away and rescuing their Christian prisoners. Even after the successful completion of this deed, despite the fact that the blows struck seem to resemble those of the old William she knew, Guiburc still requires close inspection of the hero's nose before she allows him to enter. The poet records William's exasperation upon entering in v. 2328: "Grant piece est qu'il i volsist estre." The editor might well have put an exclamation mark at the end of this line.

Mediaeval criticism being what it is, the question will likely be asked why, in view of the similarity of the porter scenes in the *Chanson de Willame* and *Aliscans,* the one in the former should be regarded as typical of Guiburc the critic of her husband while the *Aliscans* scene is serious and consonant with the traditional view of William as epic hero. An examination of the *Aliscans* situation reveals several striking differences in tone as well as event. If a brief summation will be permitted: (1) William is known to have borrowed Saracen clothes and the porter's hesitation in admitting him is justified; (2) Guiburc has good reason for not opening the gate; the ladies within have all sent their husbands with William and no gate will be opened until William returns (vv. 1623-33); William weeps at the thought of the lamentation to come; (3) The request to see William's face is made first and while William is unlacing his helmet Guiburc sees the Christian prisoners among the Saracen host and dispatches this claimant to prove himself by rescuing them (vv. 1665-80); (4) The Saracens flee thinking that this terrible man is Aarofle, angry with them for having failed to come to the field of Archamp; William performs truly mighty deeds among them and is admitted by Guiburc without more ado (vv. 1704-70); (5) Guiburc explains her predicament to William who regards her situation sympathetically. (vv. 1804-21) Compare now the situation in the *Chanson de Willame,* where William's reception at the gate has already been prepared by the previous porter scene intended to give Guiburc occasion to speak disparagingly of William's success: (1) Guiburc says that this is not the way her hero husband would return home; no mention is made anywhere of a legitimate excuse for failing to recognize William; (2) she sends the stranger off to prove himself; (3) even after the "proof," she still requires him to bare his face so that she may recognize him. Further, the dutiful wife looks after William's horse (the porter has somehow disappeared) and then proceeds to drag out of him the story of the awful defeat of the second army. The situation in the *Aliscans* is well motivated and consistent with William as conqueror and Guiburc as a cautious and reasonable woman. This external motivation is lacking in the *Chanson de Willame* version and we must needs look to the disgusted and disappointed Guiburc for internal motivation. William's mighty deeds fail to convince her of his identity, since she still insists on seeing his face before allowing him to enter. Manifestly, she did not expect such prompt and warlike action from her hesitant and incompetent husband.

It does not seem amiss to conclude that Guiburc's character is modeled less on the noble chatelaine of the *chanson de geste* than on a satirical model of the "advisor;" Guiburc is to William a parody of what Naimes is to Charlemagne in, say, *Huon de Bordeaux*. Her thoughts and reactions are very human as she laments the slaughtered knights as so many good men lost to this world. Dutifully, she serves her husband in his own field of endeavour and tries to keep him true to his purpose and duty while providing him with the means to do so. However, for a mediaeval baron, William commands very little respect at home.

He is comforted, massaged, fed, put to bed, but he has his thinking done for him. Guiburc would seem almost the ideal wife for a soldier in the several roles she manages to combine. At once she is wife, mother, recruiting officer, propaganda minister, adviser, political strategist and finally diplomat. However, William has to pay a price for all these services, one scarcely consistent with his role as conquering hero, as he smarts under the sharp tongue and bears with patience the critical word. The *Chanson de Willame* is largely concerned with William's failure to perform under these favourable circumstances, with Guiburc's reactions and with the ultimate rescue of William's reputation by two unchivalric figures.

If there is any field at all in which William excels, it is at the table. Guiburc remarks on two important occasions that an enormous appetite is the sign of William's lineage and symbolizes the strong knight figure who will wage rude warfare against his neighbour and never flee the field of battle. The first occasion is the enormous meal that Girard does justice to after reporting the plight of Vivien (vv. 1054-61). The same terms are used later with some embellishment as Guiburc marvels at the capacity of William himself:

> Qui mangue un grant pain a tamis,
> E pur ço ne laisse les dous gasteals rostiz,
> E tut mangue un grant braun porcin,
> E en aproef un grant poun rosti,
> E a dous traiz beit un sester de vin,
> Ben dure guere deit rendre a sun veisin;
> Ja trop vilment ne deit de chanp fuir
> Ne sun lingage par lui estre plus vil.
>
> (vv. 1425-32)

Eating seems to be a major preoccupation of Guiburc, or possibly it is just an example of the fact that life must continue, for her immediate response to William's plight after his second defeat at Archamp is to invite him to wash up and eat. She adds, thinking of her wasted preparations,

> Des hui matin le t'ai fait apareiller.
> Aver en poez a quatre mil chevaler
> E as serganz, e a tuz les esquiers.
>
> (vv. 2379-81)

Gui, however, finds the knightly habit of eating to be poor training for the rigours of the battlefield as he laments the practice to which Guiburc has introduced him:

> Mar vi Guiburc qui suef me norist,
> Qui me soleit faire disner si matin!
> (vv. 1737-38)

In the end, eating does not turn out to be so knightly a preoccupation after all. Rainouart, whose qualifications as a soldier appeared suspect to William because "Ben semblez home qui tost voille digner" (v. 2658), turns out to be a lover of *la bonne chère*. In the midst of battle, his thoughts are on his stomach:

> Si jo fusse a Loun la cité,
> En la cuisine u jo soleie converser,
> A cest hure me fuisse jo dignez;
> Del bon vin cler eusse beu assez.
> Si m'en dormisse juste le feu suef.
> Ço comparunt Sarazin e Escler!
> (vv. 3000-05)

Even on this trivial level, Rainouart proves himself the equal of the French chivalry.

For the sake of completeness and to clear up a little the meaning of vv. 2804-05 which the latest editor (with ample precedent) has settled on as a *locus desperatus*,[33] we may observe Guiburc's reaction to the excuse which William fabricates for Louis' absence from the field at Archamp. Ashamed to admit to Guiburc that Louis is not acting like a true epic leader, and

---

[33] McMillan, ed., *La Chanson de Guillaume*, II, 150-51. M. Yves Lefèvre has preceded me in the clarification of these lines ("Les vv. 2802-06 de la *Chanson de Guillaume* et le sens du mot *vers*," *Romania*, LXXVII (1956), 499-502) but it will be noticed that our interpretations differ. I quote his: "Guillaume suit Guiburc dans son blâme et prononce sur Louis une phrase qui, par une excuse trop visiblement feinte, stigmatise et résume incapacité de l'empereur... Le v. 2803 représente donc une invention de Guillaume: c'est une excuse bienveillante, mais trop évidemment mensongère pour que Guiburc puisse s'y laisser prendre, ou plutôt, sous la forme d'une excuse dérisoire, une cruelle satire destinée à expliquer la présente défection de l'empereur par son éternel caractère d'hésitation et d'ingratitude envers celui à qui il doit son trône." (p. 501)

seeking to defend him or, more properly, to excuse him, William says "Malade gist a sa chapele a Es." (v. 2803) Guiburc's response is:

> ... Cest vers avez vus fait.
> S'il ore gist ja ne releve il mes.
>
> (vv. 2804-05)

I translate these lines as "You have made up this little story (to deceive me); If he is really lying (ill at Aix), may he never get up again!" William mutters a hasty "Ne voille Deu...," embarrassed that Guiburc has seen through the deception, and that she does not hesitate to say so.

WILLIAM IN BATTLE: THE GUI EPISODES

H. A. Smith's interpretation of the Gui episodes in the *Chanson de Willame*[34] come the closest to making sense. "The tone and incidents of the Gui episodes are entirely in keeping with those later outgrowths of the epic, the *Enfances*..." This series of episodes, according to Mr. Smith, lacks "the dignity, seriousness and epic tone of the best and apparently primitive scenes of this poem." "Gui... is little or no better than Rainouart."[35] The bizarre nature of the Gui episodes would seem to have struck Mr. Smith, while critics before and after have largely been embarrassed by the presence of a character who fits but badly into the framework of a serious epic and therefore is at odds with their conception of the *Chanson de Willame*. While undoubtedly correct in his explanation of Gui as an exploitation of the *puer senex* topos,[36] M. Frappier fails to integrate this interpretation into his discussion of the *chanson*. Once again, in examining Gui, we find ourselves actually examining William of Orange himself. The principal incidents in which Gui is involved are the discussion of William's heir, Gui's arming by Guiburc, his reception at William's camp, his hunger and saving of William's

---

[34] Smith, "The Composition of the *Chanson de Willame*," pp. 91-97.
[35] Ibid., p. 94.
[36] Frappier, *Les Chansons de Geste*, etc., p. 176.

life, the pursuit of the Saracens and the killing of Deramed. In each of these episodes Gui appears as the *Wunderkind* who advises his elders and corrects their bad judgment, offers them real help, performs amazing deeds and withal makes them appear ridiculous. We must underline this last accomplishment, for the real importance of the teenage hero of these episodes is to stand in direct contrast with the celebrated William and save him now as Rainouart will save him later. Mr. Smith's judgment that Gui is "little or no better than Rainouart" may be amended to say that he is the early counterpart of Rainouart.

Gui's offer to be William's heir and protect both his estates and Guiburc is peremptorily dismissed by William with the words "Mielz vus vient, glut, en cendres a gisir." (v. 1453) As he will do again, William is uttering words which he will retract before very long. Prefacing his reply with the outraged remark "Unques mes n'oi tel!" (v. 1459, a Leitmotiv repeated later), Gui parrots the bold reply which an epic hero would be expected to make; since the death of Vivien, there is no man whom he would not (and could not) kill and then take possession of William's lands. (vv. 1461-73) Surprised and touched at such a reply, William agrees that Gui will be his heir, but for the moment he sends him back to the tender care of Guiburc where, manifestly, he belongs. The audience is left expecting something from this young fellow which he supplies in a manner which William himself least expects.

Gui's efforts to acquire arms and a horse in order to follow William betray a shrewd knowledge of his elders and a very canny exploitation of their weak points. Guiburc's objections to his departure are met with the Leitmotiv "Unc mais nen oi tel!" (v. 1533), and he proceeds directly to his reasons. The effect of his knightly desire to conquer and be worthy in his own right of the fief which William has agreed to settle upon him is soon counteracted by his willingness to learn from his elders and lie effectively about Guiburc's part in this adventure. He reserves what is perhaps his most telling argument for the last: solemnly, he assures Guiburc that William needs him; if he does not accompany William, the baron will not return from Archamp. (vv. 1537-39) One wonders with what confidence Guiburc sent William off to Archamp if she feels that sending Gui after him will help.

Surely a commentary once again on the hero's reputation at home! However, the very action falls within the definition of the *Wunderkind* motif and has the added piquancy of placing William of Orange in a rather silly position. It remains only to see whether the poet justifies the potential comedy he has arranged.

At Archamp, William is in the full flight of oratory, stirring up his troops to battle when he suddenly sees but does not recognize little Gui among the squires. His immediate reaction, calculated to amuse the troops, is to make a joke about Gui's size: "Bosoing out de homes qui ça l'ad amené!" (v. 1618) The jest turns back on William as everyone recognizes William's own nephew. William's mixed sadness and rage is quickly turned aside by Gui who recommends that William turn his anger against the Saracens. The count of Orange is placed in the position of having to make the best of a bad situation and he puts a good face on it by commending Gui for his good sense. But the *Wunderkind* returns to plague William when the latter suggests that Gui is unable to withstand the rigours of battle and that a guard of twenty men will keep watch over him. "Unc mais n'oi itel!" (v. 1648) replies Gui. There is no knightly answer for his argument that God looks after big and small. His demonstration of horsemanship recalls to William the achievements of Vivien and other members of this family. He stays, to ride on William's right hand. Laisse CXIII emphasizes the tableau of William and Gui riding side by side like other epic pairs of knights and the poet cannot withhold another parting line which is certainly no compliment to William: "Si n'i alast Gui, ne revenist Willame." (v. 1679)

The hunger episode in the midst of the battle serves two purposes. In the first instance, it reinforces the *Wunderkind* theme by reminding the audience for a moment that Gui, despite his capabilities, is still a child and does after all suffer the rigours and deprivations of battle with less stamina than the older and hardened campaigners. He fears that he will no longer be able to fight; he foresees his death that day on the field of Archamp. (vv. 1736-59) William asks Gui if he recalls the spot where they met the Saracens the previous Monday. There was one thing there that could not run away, says William, — the food! William sends his nephew off to refresh himself. The Saracens, thinking that Gui has gone to get Louis, attack William and soon the old warrior's horse is killed and he is fighting on foot. Only his coat of mail saves him as he calls on Gui who arrives refreshed in the nick of time. He charges the Saracens, calling out "Are you still alive, Uncle William?" and so fiercely does he attack them that they flee, thinking that Vivien has come back among them. "Ço fu grant miracle que nostre sire fist" (v. 1858) comments the poet rather (for us) ambiguously. Twenty thousand men flee from one.

While one hesitates to draw too much from a single episode, this much is incontrovertible. The roles have been radically reversed; Gui, though but a boy who suffers from weakness and hunger, has saved the life of the hero of *chanson* and legend. Charging in among the enemy, calling out to his Uncle William, Gui is the personification of the improbable *Wunderkind* who rescues his equally improbable uncle at the moment of crisis. The ambiguity in the identification of "nostre sire" of line 1858 must be left an open question, especially in a poem where no other instance of the *merveilleux chrétien* is to be found. Certainly the end of the episode finds William in a rather embarrassing position which the poet, as seems to be his wont, makes the most of in his final comment "E li quons Willame fud dunc punners." (v. 1857)

William, on accepting Gui's offer of his horse to facilitate the pursuit of the Saracens, is annoyed to find out about his nephew's deception and he rails against Gui, acusing him of speaking falsely of Guiburc. But Gui manages to avert any difficulties with William by saying "Unc mais n'oi tell" (v. 1876) and reminding him that he is supposed to be chasing the Saracens. The combination of William's short memory and Gui's bold reply supplies a fittingly comic introduction to the picture of William, legs almost dragging and stirrups flapping, riding across the field in pursuit of the enemy, but not riding so fast that Gui cannot keep up with him. (vv. 1880-87) The palfrey "vait mult suef amblant" (v. 1886) and William, weary from the battle, is obliged to rest his sword across the pommel of the saddle. (vv. 1884-85) Somehow the scene is not inconsistent with the figure of a warrior whose every battle is a defeat, who owes his two lost armies to his wife and his very life to a fifteen-year-old boy.

The final portion of the Gui episodes, the pursuit of the Saracens, contains the first part of another of the parallel constructions of which our poet was apparently so fond, the death of Deramed. This Saracen king, seeing William and judging him to be weak from his wounds, "se purpense de mult grant hardement." (v. 1894) He charges William who immediately raises his sword and the brave Deramed quickly slows to a walk. It is at this inconvenient moment that Gui asks for the privilege of killing Deramed. William reminds his nephew that no one, not even Louis, would dare to ask to strike a blow before William. When they meet, however, William rather botches the job, striking Deramed a glancing blow on the helmet and then cutting off his right leg at the thigh. It is Gui who subsequently administers the *coup de grâce*, cutting off Deramed's head. When William reproves him for this breach of knightly conduct, Gui replies with plain common sense that it never does to leave an enemy alive to engender heirs who could come waging war in his stead. Once again, William patronizingly praises the child who thinks like a baron. H. A. Smith [37] observed the parallel between this killing of Deramed and the killing of Alderufe. (vv. 2094-2209) It remains to determine the significance of this adaptation as we find it in the Gui episode.

Gui's performance of the *coup de grâce* on Deramed and his justification of the deed appear to be further exploits of the *Wunderkind* variety. Deramed's attempt to attack the weakened count is a near parody on the traditional pagan-Christian individual combat which the hearer recalls during the Alderufe-William struggle. The heroics of the later combat, even the actual events, lose much of their epic lustre when Deramed's cowardly attitude and Gui's example in furnishing the *coup de grâce* are recalled. The ineptitude of William, corrected and advised by a young boy, completes the parody of an otherwise stock epic situation.

The traditional interpretation of the final line of laisse CXXX "Ore out vencu sa bataille Willame" (v. 1980), has been a comparison with v. 3649 of the *Roland* "E Carles ad sa bataille ven-

---

[37] Smith, "The Composition of the *Chanson de Willame*," pp. 93-96.

cue."[38] The superficiality of this comparison is manifest in the light of the very different circumstances under which they occur. Charlemagne, speeding to his revenge despite his great age, has battered down the walls of Saragoce; Marsilie is dead; little remains but to baptize some 100,000 pagan prisoners. William, however, old and tired, has gone unwillingly to this second battle; he has lost his second army of 30,000 men; his best barons have been killed or captured; his latest exploits have been overshadowed by those of a fifteen-year-old boy whom he has recently treated with scorn. William will shortly see this young hero captured and Vivien, his best vassal, die. Far from baptizing many pagans, William has witnessed the relapse into Islam of his own adopted nephew Guischard while some 20,000 Saracens withdraw safe and sound to their ships. Exhibiting rare common sense, William ascribes Vivien's death to his senseless oath. After Gui's capture, William laments with perfect truth:

> Cum se vait declinant ma grant nobilité
> Et cum est destruit tut mun riche parenté.
> (vv. 2081-82)

As we have already noted, the poet has even arranged for the traditional clash of ideologies meeting in single combat to end badly with a decapitation scene which is only a copy of Gui's previous exploit. As other pagans come upon the scene, William departs for Orange, the pagans chasing him all the way. Considering the larger context in which it is set, "Ore out vencu sa bataille Willame" is in no way analagous to the corresponding verse of the *Chanson de Roland* except as a parody may be analagous to its object.

The Rainouart Episodes

We have already discussed the question of the composite nature of the *Chanson de Willame* and the effort hitherto put into an

---

[38] Compare the reporting of Gunter's prowess in the *Nibelungenlied*, 682, 4.

attempt to discover Rainouart's source and so discover his meaning. It is our contention, previously stated, that the source of Rainouart has nothing to do with his presence in the *Chanson de Willame*. On the contrary, the Rainouart episodes, however "unpolished" their integration into the whole *chanson* may seem, fit the meaning of the whole text as we find it: a human commentary on both the legendary William and the traditional chivalry of the *chanson de geste*. It now remains to examine these episodes in context and note the relative success with which they illustrate the central themes of the *Chanson de Willame*.

Rainouart is first of all the legendary type of the ogre. His *tinel*, too heavy for an ordinary man to carry, seems almost a magical arm, but despite Rainouart's claim that it is irreplacable (v. 2741), any magical quality about it disappears when Rainouart breaks it over the head of his uncle Aildré. (vv. 3303-04) His speed in returning to pick up the forgotten *tinel* is so great that he has returned before the French have all passed the ford they were crossing when he left. (vv. 2772-73) During the battle, Rainouart actually poles a Saracen ship with his *tinel* while Bertram steers (vv. 3057-67) and later personally kills 2,000 of the fleeing Saracens. (v. 3341) His exploits of individual combat are no less remarkable and we shall discuss their importance in a moment. Despite these marvellous deeds, whose almost supernatural character the poet has either forgotten or chosen to forget, Rainouart is a most sympathetic character. As Bédier aptly remarked, he is "très peuple." [39] His ragged and tattered appearance, his predilection for the joys of the kitchen, his enormous appetite (totally unrelated by the poet to any nobility of lineage [40]) all evidence the back stairs education of the servant. Once given the opportunity to better himself in a manner suited to his talents, Rainouart lays out his master in the fire, telling him that henceforth he may take the blame when things are stolen or botched (vv. 2690-91), and departs in William's cortege. Rainouart's troubles with the kitchen boys who get him drunk, steal his *tinel* and burn his mustache in the fire serve but to endear him to his audience. In

---

[39] Joseph Bédier, *Les légendes épiques*, 2e éd., Paris: 1914, I, 97.
[40] See pages 34-35 above.

a scene whose full comic potential is developed in the *Chanson de Willame* (vv. 3080-3122) and in *Aliscans* (vv. 5432-5569), Rainouart as ogre displays more prowess than usefulness in attempting to secure arms for the lately freed prisoners when he crushes horse and rider, armour and all, with each stroke of the *tinel*. Bertram's suggestion that he butt them with the mighty *just* is received with amazed surprise by Rainouart who plays the role of a child-like *vilain* in the scene. A jolly bit of macabre humour is the picture of Rainouart using a body for a pillow after a drunken kitchen brawl. (v. 2893) Brother to Guiburc and son of a king he may be (one doubts that the French really believe it), but he remains fundamentally a kitchen boy to the end and even beyond, if one may judge by his jest to William in the last three lines of the poem.

We have already observed that Rainouart is Gui's counterpart in the last part of the poem as the saviour of William and the real victor of the last battle of Archamp. In their first encounter, the author pursues a familiar pattern by putting into William's mouth a judgment which circumstances will shortly discredit. William's remark that Rainouart looks to be a big eater [41] and a late sleeper (vv. 2658-59), a very unlikely candidate for a military campaign, is soon contradicted when Rainouart himself rousts the knights out of bed and forces them into a march of fifteen leagues before daybreak. (vv. 2896-2919) The knights have already decided that Rainouart is mad, so eager is he for battle when their own bowels are trembling (to use the poet's own happy phrase, vv. 2785-89); they boast that they will punish him for misusing them in this fashion, but William replies very sensibly that they had best not talk, since not a man of them could do it. (vv. 2925-28) The day of the *gab* is evidently over when there is a risk of being held to it. [42]

The *gab* is not the only epic cliché debunked in the Rainouart episodes. The traditional invitation to all cowards to flee before the battle, a device usually designed to heighten the terror in the

---

[41] See pages 34-35 and 42 above.
[42] The comparison with the *Pèlerinage de Charlemagne* suggests itself immediately.

mind of the hearer, is withdrawn by Rainouart and turned to use as an effective bit of realism and a tribute to the powers of a real leader as the cowards, "encouraged" by Rainouart's *tinel*, return to fight well and prove of great service to William. (vv. 2949-83) Even as he supplied strength to the cowards, Rainouart is the mainspring of the French forces. The picture of the French chivalry finally successful under a dynamic leadership of action and example, the leadership of a *vilain*, a kitchen boy, the very antithesis of knighthood, is unmistakably a continuation of the anti-chivalric emphasis of the earlier parts of the *Chanson de Willame*. Aside from waking the sluggard knights, going before them to battle, encouraging cowards, showing in his later rebellion little respect for rank or privilege, Rainouart not only suggests to the French the strategy of destroying the enemy ships but carries out the operation himself, releasing several important captives in the process. (vv. 3006 ff.) It is in his individual combats, however, that Rainouart most notably becomes the *héros vilain*. Of the six Saracens that Rainouart personally accounts for in single combat, four are dispatched in special circumstances. After Malagant (vv. 3135-37) and Gloriant de Palerne (vv. 3157-62), Rainouart slays Tabur de Canaloine (vv. 3170-3201), a hard-shelled, long-toothed, hairy pagan whose teeth and nails (his only arms) serve to terrorize the French and whose tough hide has resisted the swords of William and two others. William personally appeals to Rainouart to slay the terrible *amirail* Balan (vv. 3208-67) which he accomplishes by wearing the armour of seven men. Rainouart's uncle Aildré comes looking for William and the giant protects his patron by saying that he is dead and engaging the Saracen himself, breaking his *tinel* over Aildré's head. (vv. 3273-3304) Finally recalling the sword at his side, Rainouart slays the king Foré with it, passing a comment that one should always carry four of these useful little weapons about in order to have spares. (vv. 3305-33) Against this record, the one line devoted to William's prowes ("Mult i feri ben Willame al curb niés" v. 2984) appears formal indeed.

The triumph of the servant lad is complete. Thrice he saves his patron, once without William's knowledge. Rejecting the trappings of chivalry, remaining loyal to his kitchen upbringing, employing lower class means more effectively in a traditionally upper class situation, appealing, in a word, to an audience long since saturated with the improbabilities of chivalry, the *vilanus vindicatus* brings this anti-*chanson de geste* to a satisfyingly successful conclusion. Comedy, parody, bourgeois common sense and commentary on a dead convention are not finely distinguished, but rather cemented together by a tale filled with excitement, suspense, drama, villains and powerful deeds which elicit from the hearer an involuntary involvement that only the comic and the grotesque can break through. In Rainouart the author of our *chanson de geste* has found the perfect hero for the final victory which chivalry was no longer able to supply but which the audience demanded. The observation may be permitted that it is less important to know from which hypothetical "original" Rainouart came than to understand what he represents.

The Qualities of Chivalry

It seems clear from our examination of the *Chanson de Willame* that it deals specifically with certain qualities and capabilities of the epic knight as exemplified by William and the characters around him. They might briefly be designated as "knighthood" (valour, prowess in battle, high-mindedness), "generalship" (strategical ability, leadership, influence) and "intelligence" (determination and foresight with a touch of cunning). All of them are not, to be sure, necessary to the satisfactory knight who may well get along with only the first category, but they are all necessary to a baron of William's stature. Like Arthur, Gunther, King Mark and Charlemagne, William as leader should sum up the ideal of epic achievement, while leaving most of the achieving to be done by the knights.[43] Like the Charlemagne of the *Chanson de Roland*,

---

[43] The concept of kingship in both epic and courtly literature has been a subject for discussion which could be enlarged upon. The relevant point at this juncture would be the king or equivalent leader as ideal source of knightly qualities and capabilities versus the relative inactivity of the leader in fact. Exceptions to this are William in the *Chanson de Willame* and Charlemagne in the *Baligant* episode of the *Roland*, where the leader attempts to act with varying degrees of success. Manifestly, this question requires much room and consideration and I offer the present comparison only as an interesting possibility.

however, William emerges from his court to face the test of action. To observe that he is found wanting is to leave the picture incomplete, for the qualities he lacks are made up by those around him. In a sense, then, William would have done well to emulate his various followers. An examination and recapitulation of these characters reveal, however, that William is likely better off (in human terms) not possessing these qualities, at least in the manner and to the extent that his followers possess them.

Vivien more than anyone else typifies the true knight and chivalric leader. While his feats are of a general nature, no one could say that the general run of knights in the *Chanson de Willame* demonstrate an eagerness or fitness for battle comparable to his. While the early armies apparently do go willingly to the slaughter, Vivien has some difficulty keeping his troops on the battlefield and the army assembled at Laon is scarcely brimming with enthusiasm. Their bowels tremble at the thought of strife and they require the constant "encouragement" of Rainouart's *tinel* to keep them moving. Vivien, on the other hand, has been trained in an idealism unshakable even in the face of certain disaster. While admirable as a single knight, Vivien fails as a general in sacrificing strategy to the pursuit of his knightly code. His concept of generalship consists of promising to call for William, calling for him too late, standing and admiring the enemy while they charge and returning to the battle time and again against hopeless odds. Again, we have already observed the extent to which Vivien not only typifies the epic knight but is burdened with every epic cliché to be found in the *Chanson de Roland*.[44] It is thus that the epitome becomes a caricature. While we may grieve for Vivien's disaster, William makes the point clear by blaming him for his blind fulfillment of his oath. Vivien has perished, but William survives to fight another time and, ultimately, to win. Nor does William err in the other extreme exemplified by the anti-knight and anti-general Tedbalt with his companion Esturmi. If the latter are indeed anti-heroes, drunken, inexperienced and cowardly, given the command of better men through the vagaries of the feudal system, the men who follow them to battle receive little better

---

[44] See pages 25-26 above.

treatment when they follow the valiant into battle. However, William remains in the middle of the two extremes. Obviously, he is better off than Tedbalt and Esturmi, but is he not also and does he not admit to being bettter off for having avoided the excesses of Vivien? It does not seem unreasonable to see here an attitude typical of an audience familiar with the disparities between knightly conduct and the realities of the battlefield. William at least appears as a figure with whom they can identify: incompetent (except in the stock situation, sword in hand), but sensible and brave enough for one man.

At this juncture we may perhaps consider William's anger at the court of Louis. Perhaps more than anything else, this scene serves to bring William closer to the hearts of his audience, revealing him as a blunt and, when he chooses to be, coarse man who is not averse to lapsing into the language of the soldiery among whom he has spent his life. However interesting and even convincing may be explanatory pronouncements on the *moeurs* of another age less sensitive to forthright and even crude language and less considerate of certain delicacies in the presence of ladies, one must indeed stretch credence a little to find William's language to the queen completely consonant with the conduct of an ideal epic baron. When the queen accuses Guiburc of being a pagan poisoner and William of plotting the death of Louis so that he may seize the throne, William's reply leaves one a trifle breathless. The relevant lines are 2598-2624. The atmosphere is rather that of the *fabliau* than the *chanson de geste*. A prudish scholarship, evidently regarding this action as a most regrettable relapse on the conqueror's part, has resisted discussion of this sorry burst of temper which would spoil the picture of the perfect baron that critical commentary has so carefully nurtured in the *Chanson de Willame*. M. Frappier remarks only that "Les scènes de Laon, probablement abrégées dans G^2, gagnent beaucoup à être lues dans la version *d'Aliscans*." [45] However, M. Frappier fails completely to discuss the episode in the *Chanson de Willame* and thus does not mention the complete difference in tone between the *Aliscans* version where William's anger is truly that of

---

[45] Frappier, *Les Chanson de Geste*, etc., p. 219.

an outraged noble cruelly rejected by a timorous and feeble king and our version which offers a much less able William dealing with a viper-tongued queen in the manner of a Billingsgate fishwife.

Guiburc's qualities of foresight and determination are admirable and certainly as exceptional as her skill as an often sarcastic critic. She tempers these qualities with a cunning that speaks volumes, however, as she stoops to patent falsehood. The encouragements which she holds out to the second army are not those which Vivien would have mentioned in her place: service of God, country, and liege lord, revenge for the slaughter of noble knights, glory, opportunity to prove one's arms, eternal salvation as the reward of courageous death. She is naturally forced to mention the death of Vivien and she adds the traditional praise:

> Mieldre vassal ne pout estre né
> Pur eshalcer la sainte crestienté
> Ne pur lei maintenir ne garder.
> (vv. 1375-77)

But then she promises them booty from the damaged ships with token resistance from only 10,000 pagans, generous gifts from William, and a beautiful wife should they require encouragement to acquire so much land. William is weak and encourages the easiest line. He even tries it himself but, typically, fails miserably in the attempt. Before speaking to his troops at the third battle of Archamp, William carefully divides his troops into the landed nobles and the landless and then speaks differently to each class. To the landed gentry he gives assurances that he seeks no material gain from their death but that he will augment their holdings, protect their heirs, and even increase their heirs' holdings if they be small. (vv. 1565-82) "Fel seit Willame, s'il unques en out dener!" he cries in v. 1581. The landed swear loyalty and William moves over to the landless. Recalling the terrible things that Deramed has done, William says that now he has here against Deramed the best force of men ever assembled. Only Louis could assemble better, says he, adding that he only makes this concession because, as he modestly observes, "Encuntre lui ne me dei pas vanter." (v. 1609) William is heaping praise on his knights of no economic standing, recalling their importance to the battle:

> Ja n'ert ben faite grant bataille chanpel,
> Se vavassurs ne la funt endurer,
> E ne la meintenent les legers bachelers,
> Les forz, les vigrus, les hardiz, les menbrez
> (vv. 1611-14)

when he catches sight of Gui and cracks the joke that rebounds on him to the detriment of his oratory.[46] William fails to complete his job of arousing his men to action by means that are more traditional though less overtly deceptive than Guiburc's. Once again he fails to fall into either mold of deception and is the better off for it in the eyes of the audience whose reactions to both ploys would doubtless betray their familiarity. His negative qualities assume a positive flavour in this regard, since Guiburc and William present a caricature rather than play a role and the question is still whether general human incompetence is preferred to such a caricature.

Rainouart is indeed a caricature. In reading the account of the last battle of Archamp, one has the impression that not much is going on except the marvellous deeds of the giant kitchen boy. Only he ever truly accomplishes the work of the epic knight or reaches his prized goal: single combat with the most illustrious or the fiercest of the enemy knights and victory over all of them. But in Rainouart's case, the whole matter is exaggerated. For Rainouart, primitive brute strength personified, the cost is not great; he is never injured, he only breaks his *tinel*. No fewer than six kings (each with a terrible peculiarity) and several thousand lesser pagans succumb to his efforts. His evident joy and completely pleasant and carefree manner make the whole process seem like a high school lark — a position reinforced by his comment in the last lines of the poem, "If I had known you were my brother-in-law, William, I would have been more use to you at Archamp." (vv. 3552-54) The whole situation is familiar: "Place

---

[46] See page 38 above.

aux laquais!" So a caricature of knightly prowess and raw courage saves William when chivalry has failed.

William's position is an unenviable one. As leader, he is supposed to possess the range of qualities from Vivien through Guiburc and Gui to Rainouart. Manifestly, did he possess them as the others do, he would finish up as a caricature of caricatures. This is precisely the reason why William the ideal baron is an impossible figure. As an ideal leader he exists only in legend as do Arthur, Gunther, Mark and to a large extent Charlemagne. In the *Chanson de Willame* he exists as a man among men. The audience can understand and sympathize with his poor performance and limited capabilities and yet still admire his efforts and what prowess he is able to show on the field as he does his best to live up to a scale of values which the late twelfth—century audience could be sure never existed.

The Literary Value of the "Chanson de Willame"

It has been customary among critics of the *Chanson de Willame* to add a measure of "appreciation" or some comment on the "literary value" of the poem to whatever other comments they may have made. Mr. F. W. Nachtmann's concise summary [47] of these judgments relieves us of the task of outlining them. Suffice it to say that they run the full range of the spectrum from Ferdinand Lot: "Littérairement c'est sans doute la plus belle de nos chansons de geste," [48] to E. R. Curtius: "a witless, inferior minstrel." [49] The observations ranging in between betray a surprising divergence of opinion which Mr. Nachtmann has observed and commented upon most aptly.

> As to whether the poem is a work of art, the decision varies with the standards of the critic and his viewpoint. The majority of the important scholars have considered

---

[47] Nachtmann, *A History of Studies of the Old French William Cycle*, pp. 168-73.
[48] Lot, *Etudes*, etc., p. 243.
[49] E. R. Curtius, "Über die altfranzösische Epik," *Zeitschrift für Romanische Philologie*, LXIV (1944), 289.

the poem as a work of art. There is obviously a general correlation between the belief in the poem's antiquity and its literary beauty: i.e., the critics who are most emphatic in claiming great age for the *Chanson de Guillaume* are also emphatic in claiming great literary quality for it. Becker, however, is a notable exception. [50]

It is a fair observation that age is poor grounds for judging the literary value of anything. It is also possible that the importance of the *Chanson de Guillaume* as the kingpin of theories on the William of Orange cycle in most critical opinion has become confused with any artistic value it might have. To judge of the strictness of criteria involved in most such evaluations, we have but to observe the conclusion of M. Frappier which Mr. Nachtmann recommends for "its recency and the authority of its author:" [51]

> ... un caractère de grandeur égal à celui du *Roland* d'Oxford; celui-ci a sans nul doute servi de modèle, mais l'imitation a été originale, a produit une tonalité neuve: art plus rude et plus raide, moins calculé, contrastes abrupts du sublime et d'un réalisme volontiers truculent, poésie plus sauvage, pathétique âpre d'une singulière puissance. Oui, le manuscrit de Londres, dans une forme assez misérable, a sauvé un poème d'une magnifique inspiration. [52]

We may certainly agree with Mr. Frappier on the "tonalité neuve" while disputing that the poetry is "plus raide, moins calculé ... plus sauvage," since at least the last two of these judgments accord ill with the poem as we have analysed it and Mr. Frappier presents no detailed analysis of the language of the poem to substantiate his statements. Our point is that criticism has hitherto been involved with the importance of the poem in its position among other *chansons de geste* and has restricted judgment on its artistic value to a somewhat impressionistic statement of its "style." Without abandoning the position that evaluation is not

---

[50] Nachtmann, *A History*, etc., p. 174.
[51] *Ibid.*, p. 172.
[52] Frappier, *Les Chansons de Geste*, etc., p. 150.

the first interest of criticism, we may at least attempt a few statements.

Throughout this discussion we have used the words "bourgeois audience," "common-sense attitudes," "experience" versus "traditional." We have mentioned the *fabliau* atmosphere. One hesitates to overlay literary criticism with sociological considerations, but the text seems clear. Far from being the oldest *chanson de geste* or the source or even an integral part of the cycle of William of Orange, the *Chanson de Willame,* presenting William as an anti-conqueror, as a demonstration of human limitations, is an atypical epic. As a restatement of human values outside the stylized tradition of the epic, it effectively serves to debunk in some measure the sterile repetition of the perennially heroic and improbable deeds of a mythical chivalry long gone in the days of Chrétien de Troyes. We may therefore reasonably conclude that, having been removed from under the shadow of the *Chanson de Roland,* it need no longer be considered either a paler repetition of the traditional values or an *excitatorium* to war against the pagans, but can stand on its own as an entertaining piece of mediaeval literature.

www.ingramcontent.com/pod-product-compliance
Lightning Source LLC
Chambersburg PA
CBHW020423230426
43663CB00007BA/1285